S0-BHX-418

WILD Horses
Endangered Beauty

WILD Horses
Endangered Beauty

traer scott

MERRELL
LONDON · NEW YORK

For my brother John, whose innate empathy and compassion have always been an inspiration to me. Always remember that true strength comes in many forms.

INTRODUCTION

From the very beginning, I have been, at best, a dilettante when it comes to horses. As a kid, I could distinguish at least a hundred different breeds of dog, but as to horses, I knew only three things: that they were much bigger in real life than in my imagination, that they involved a lot of work, and that somewhere out there existed a spectacular thing called a wild mustang. I was about six when I became fascinated with horses. Like many little girls, I found a certain romantic power and beauty in the idea of riding a horse at full gallop across a foggy moor, like a heroine in a novel. My parents, who dutifully indulged my various obsessions, enrolled me in riding lessons at a stable near our semi-rural home. We had to drive down a dirt lane to get there. The old road was always thick with red clay dust, which billowed in through the open windows of our air-conditionless Opel wagon, causing my mother to curse most of the way to my lessons.

I had the crop, the hat, and even the riding pants, but the reality of horses began to sink in when I spent more than half of my first lesson learning the very boring, hairy art of grooming. I lived in North Carolina and even then, when most roads outside the city limit were either dirt or newly paved, I understood there would be no romantic galloping with a velvet cape flying behind me. Still, I pressed on because what I really, really wanted was to win a ribbon. Alas, after a few months, I was found to be severely allergic to horses. I broke out in hives, my throat closing ominously, every time I was in a barn or got horse hair on my skin. This put an abrupt end to my horse dreams and, instead, I turned my attention to making my cocker spaniel into a champion show dog. Nonetheless, before my early retirement, I somehow managed to participate in a horse show, in which I won what I can only assume was a participation ribbon (pink, in my case) given out to young children so they would feel some sense of accomplishment and want to buy more lessons. I hung it proudly on my wall and fell asleep at night with my attention alternating between *Champion Dog: Prince Tom* (the classic 1955 story of an underdog who becomes a world champion) and *Misty of Chincoteague*.

Misty of Chincoteague by Marguerite Henry, first published in 1947, has been an extremely popular children's book for more than sixty years. It is based on the true story of a family's attempts to raise a wild pony, and, like generations of other kids, I was entranced by the idea of the untamable spirit of the wild horse. Oddly enough, though, I was in my twenties before I managed to figure out that Chincoteague was in fact very close to where I had lived as a child, and that, furthermore, one of the oldest bands of wild horses in existence lived—and still lives—on the chain of islands off North Carolina known as the Outer Banks.

This is somewhat indicative of many people's knowledge of the wild horse. When I mentioned to people the work I was doing on this book, I almost invariably got the same response. Most folks (particularly women) would sigh, eyes glazing over as if they had drifted off to some fantastic daydream at the mere mention, and softly utter "Ohhh, wild horses." I came to realize that most people think—as I had done—either that wild horses are marvelous but unreal creatures that live only in folklore, or that they are still flourishing, running free in large numbers "elsewhere." The truth lies somewhere between the two.

In fact, today there are more "wild" horses in captivity than in the wild. The majority (around 30,000, though estimates differ) are in government holding facilities, while thousands more live in sanctuaries or have been adopted into private ownership. Those that still "run free" are either in government-controlled public lands or in dedicated areas (nature preserves) with natural or man-made boundaries to protect them from getting hit by cars, shot at, or fed sandwiches by tourists.

The ongoing history of the American mustang is long and complex, and a brief historical overview is crucial to understanding our horses' current perilous and uncertain future. "Mustang" derives from the Spanish term *mestengo*, meaning a stray or feral beast, and in fact the mustang is a feral horse rather than a truly wild horse ("feral" is the word used to describe once-domestic animals that have turned to living wild). It is now believed that the horse originated approximately 50 million years ago on the North American continent, as the spaniel-sized, four-toed *Eohippus*, and gradually evolved to become the plains-dwelling, uncloven-hoofed *Equus caballus* about 2 million years ago. *Equus* migrated across the Bering Strait to Asia, where it was first domesticated by humans. It became extinct in America during or just after the last ice age, around 10,000 years ago, for reasons that are not clear. In the fifteenth and sixteenth centuries, the Spanish conquistadores brought horses with them to the New World, and in this way the animals were reintroduced to the continent. The first arrived with Christopher Columbus on his second voyage, to the West Indies, in 1493, while the first to reach the mainland were brought by Hernán Cortés in 1519.

Many of these Spanish horses escaped or were stolen or bartered by the Native Americans, who took to the horse with an amazing naturalness and used it for hunting (in particular buffalo), transportation, trading, and battle. Some Native Americans became great horsemasters and engaged in selective breeding to improve desirable traits. As time went on, other horses not of Spanish ancestry escaped from, or were deliberately released by, among others, ranchers, explorers, and the cavalry to join the free-roaming herds. The gene pool was expanded, and by the end of the nineteenth century there were an estimated 2 million feral horses in North America, mostly concentrated in the Southwest.

That's a lot of horses, and it is perhaps not surprising that the mustangs were viewed as an inexhaustible resource to be used and, of course, abused. The herds were hunted for sport, for the meat industry (pet food in particular), and for use by the military. Hunting methods were often ferocious and inhumane, involving horses being chased by airplanes, driven over cliffs to their death, corralled and slaughtered en masse, or poisoned at their watering holes. It was such practices as these that in 1952 led Velma Johnston—who would become known as "Wild Horse Annie"—to embark on an impassioned campaign in protest against the inhumane treatment of the feral herds. Wild Horse Annie's lobbying resulted first in the banning of the use of airplanes for the pursuit of wild horses in Storey County, Nevada; but that was only the beginning. Bringing the plight of the mustangs to the attention of Congress, she continued her crusade against cruel practices until in 1971 a federal law was passed, the Wild Free-Roaming Horse and Burro Act, enshrining the place of the feral horse in American history and proclaiming that "wild free-roaming horses and burros are living symbols of the historic and pioneer spirit of the West; that they contribute to the diversity of life forms within the Nation and enrich the lives of the American people; and that these horses and burros are fast disappearing from the American scene . . . ."

The Bureau of Land Management (BLM) is tasked with managing most of the remaining herds; this mainly consists of the removal of wild horses and burros from public lands. The horses compete with cattle for grazing land and, not bringing any income to ranchers, are held to be nothing more than pests. Maintaining a balance between the needs of domestic livestock, wild horses, and the environment is a delicate and thorny issue. Today, just 22,000 mustangs (according to recent estimates; exact numbers are not known) roam government-managed lands in the states of Arizona, California, Colorado, Idaho, Montana, Nevada, New Mexico, Oregon, Utah, and Wyoming—more than in the wild. There are also prominent privately managed herds in North Carolina, Maryland, and Virginia. (By contrast, some 6 million cattle and other private livestock are grazed on public lands.) Once removed from the wild by the BLM, the horses are kept in holding facilities and then offered for sale to the public in adoption auctions. In these auctions, the winning bidder is allowed to adopt a horse but will not receive full title ownership until one year later. This waiting period is meant not simply to ensure that the adopter knows how to care properly for the horse but also to act as a disincentive against selling the horse for an immediate profit, especially to a slaughterhouse; one year's worth of time and resources is an investment that will not be recouped by selling the horse for meat.

Although the act of 1971 was intended to protect America's wild mustangs, animal welfare enthusiasts maintain that it has been undermined through the decades by subsequent amendments as well as by questionable removal practices. It is estimated that less than 25 percent of the mustang population of 1971 remains today. One piece of controversial legislation was the Burns Amendment, which was introduced by Senator Conrad Burns of Montana and quietly tacked on to the 2005 Federal Appropriations Bill. The amendment mandated the BLM to sell wild horses over the age of ten, and those that had been passed over three times for adoption, at livestock auctions, where they are likely to be sold to slaughterhouses. These "kill auctions," as they are often called, are open to the public, and the highest bidder is often a meat buyer who sells horses or other livestock to slaughter. Not all horses sold at livestock auctions end up at slaughter—some are purchased by horse traders or bargain hunters—but it is a dangerous gamble, and the animal often loses.

The fact that wild mustangs were being rounded up and killed to satisfy demands for horse meat for human consumption caused a huge public outcry. Unfortunately, it is a sad fact that upwards of 100,000 unwanted domestic horses are still sold to slaughter every year, although the realities of the horse-meat market have always been hidden from horse-loving Westerners. Owing to state legislation we have recently seen the closing of the last horse-slaughter plants in the United States, but horses are simply being exported for slaughter to plants in Canada and Mexico.

The American Horse Slaughter Prevention Act (H.R. 503/S.311) would prohibit any American horses, domestic or wild, from being slaughtered within the country for human consumption or from being shipped out of the country for that purpose. This bill passed the House of Representatives in 2006 in a landslide, bipartisan vote of 263–146, but failed to pass in the Senate. The bill is set to be re-introduced in the next Congressional Session, giving Congress another chance to pass the American Horse Slaughter Prevention Act. Until it does, mustangs (and all other horses) still face the looming threat of the slaughterhouse, where death is anything but humane.

As we have seen, these inspiring, intelligent, and tenacious animals have populated our continent for centuries, often in a fruitful partnership with humans. Yet after tractors replaced horsepower, public opinion turned and the wild horse began to be seen as more of a nuisance than a resource. The main problem facing the mustangs is that they belong both to no one and to everyone. They are, quite literally, living history, with rare or unique bloodlines preserved in their herds. Now, however, they are essentially unprofitable and often (though by no means always) take up land that could otherwise be used for grazing livestock or for development. With the exception of coastal areas that reap tourism money from visitors wishing to see the horses, they provide no substantial income and exist just for the sake of existing—which should, perhaps, carry more innate value than it does. As it is, the Colonial Spanish Mustang is listed as critically endangered by both the American Livestock Breeds Conservancy and the Equus Survival Trust.

Mustangs arrive at sanctuaries in various ways. Some come from the different government agencies responsible for the management of wild horses in an effort to prevent them from being sent to a kill auction. Others are purchased directly from those public auctions to keep them from going to buyers who sell unwanted horses to slaughterhouses for profit. Still other horses are surrendered by their owners, who may have adopted or purchased them and realized only later that they are unable to care for them. In some cases, sanctuaries take in horses that have been seized from neglectful or abusive situations.

In making this book, I traveled to several different regions that to me best represent the various modern states of the wild horse. I first visited Lompoc, California, spending almost a week at the Return to Freedom American Wild Horse Sanctuary, where hundreds of rescued mustangs and burros (as well as some domestics) live on a beautiful, sprawling 300-acre (120-hectare) ranch. Here, a small, dedicated staff managed by ex-Hollywood prop and wardrobe stylist Neda DeMayo cares for the horses, works to preserve rare mustang bloodlines, and tirelessly educates the public about the threats facing wild horses and burros.

As I drove down the long track to the Return to Freedom ranch in my red Mustang convertible (by a happy quirk of fate, the rental company in Santa Barbara had run out of compacts), I was greeted by Jasper, a charming and very vocal older male burro. He stuck his head right in at my window, which was slightly unnerving, but he quickly became a favorite of mine. Burros are rather like big, hoofed dogs. They're curious and like to follow you

around, and they love treats and a good cuddle. Jasper roams freely around the sanctuary, which also houses dozens of other rescued burros, and often brays loudly at passersby, dogs, and other animals. The sleek, graceful horses tend to get all the glory, but it was actually the highly intelligent, sensitive burros that I fell in love with at Return to Freedom. Just like mustangs, burros are available for adoption through both BLM and private programs. I can't wait until I have more land; I want to wake up to burros.

Despite the January weather, which made for cool, sunny days but very muddy grounds, my experience at Return to Freedom was invigorating. Shannon Schureman, a southern California college student and lifelong rider and equine enthusiast, was staying at the ranch as a volunteer, and graciously spent every day helping me in this project. In between the frosty, foggy dawn, when she got up to help feed the herds, and the last chores before the colorful California sunset, she escorted me around the property, introduced me to the many horses, helped me with terminology, and ensured that I didn't get kicked or stampeded because of my lack of "horse sense." What amazed me the most about my initial immersion in the world of horses was how social they are. Return to Freedom was the first sanctuary to focus on rescuing entire family bands. Its efforts are evident in every corner of the sanctuary, where mothers, babies, siblings, and bonded herds are inseparable, clearly thriving on something akin to the emotional comfort we derive from sharing our lives with loved ones. Seeing this made me

Shannon Schureman, a volunteer at Return to Freedom Sanctuary in California, nuzzles a horse.

realize even more how destructive indiscriminate government round-ups can be, particularly when such bands as these are broken up and the horses separated, often permanently, from their families and herds.

Lifesavers Wild Horse Rescue is also based in California, at two locations: the Born to Be Wild sanctuary in extremely rural Kern County and a ranch in the desert town of Lancaster, about two hours north of Los Angeles. Leaving Return to Freedom on a warm, sunny day, I drove my Mustang, top down (with a scarf tied around my hair à la Grace Kelly), for four hours along narrow mountain roads with hairpin turns, through vast corporate farming lands, past small villages inhabited by Mexican migrant workers, and finally through an imposing canyon peppered with free-range cattle, which often stood and blocked the road. Jill Starr's Born to Be Wild mustang sanctuary is here in the arid mountains of Twin Oaks, near Caliente, about an hour and a half south of Bakersfield.

At the 160-acre (65-hectare) sanctuary, horses that have difficulty adjusting to humans or have been mistreated lead a tranquil life that imitates the ways of their wild heritage as much as possible. A long dirt road runs through the sanctuary, and on either side, bands of horses are kept in enormous habitats with fields, shady trees, and rocky hills to explore. Human intervention is avoided except when needed to maintain proper health.

Halfway down the dirt road I came across Cowboy, a young beef steer with no ears, adopted by Jill and her husband. As a baby, Cowboy had his ears chewed off by another animal, rendering him completely deaf. Now safe from accidents, further mutilation, and the slaughterhouse, he hangs out on the property, acting as an alert but slow-moving sentinel at the entrance to the horse habitats.

On the second day I was there, Jill had to remove a horse (in order to administer medicine) from the largest band, while trying to avoid a mass escape by the others. In the attempt, three horses did in fact manage to break out. At first, the trio galloped excitedly down the road toward the gate, enjoying the rare opportunity to be on the other side of the fence, but within a few minutes they had all drifted back down to the herd and were nuzzling their companions through the fence. Although they were easily spooked, making it difficult to get them back through the correct gate, they clearly felt ill at ease being separated, even briefly, from the other horses.

Just after dawn, when feeding began, the herd often galloped up and down the field in anticipation. This was my first experience of being in the middle of twenty or so very fast, extremely large, powerful moving animals. I was frightened and overwhelmed, but tried to remember that horses are prey animals and will therefore almost always choose flight over fight. When one would get too near to me, I "got big" by putting my hands up over my head, which makes them turn and run. This was one of the first lessons I learned on this trip, and it came in handy many times.

The Lancaster ranch is in the middle of the desert, not far from Edwards Air Force Base. At the ranch, suitable mustangs are "gentled" (acclimated to being touched by people and, eventually, harnessed and ridden) as part of their adoption process. Responsible candidates who meet a range of criteria are able to adopt a beautiful gentled mustang for an affordable price, which in turn helps support the rescue of more horses. The ranch is open to the public, tours are offered, and there is a fantastic little gift shop that offers exceptionally fun and unique horse-themed items from around the world.

Once again, it was deemed that I should have some company, since it is almost impossible to be completely alert to your wider surroundings while looking through a lens. Martin Vilmer, a sixteen-year-old Lifesavers volunteer and son of assistant manager Chris Vilmer, had a broken arm resulting from a recent riding accident, leaving him at leisure to pal around with me for the day. Martin suggested I kneel inside a large, hard plastic feed bin in one of the 20-acre (8-hectare) corrals while the herd galloped back and forth. It was a rare opportunity—as both a photographer and an animal lover—to be right in among dozens of galloping mustangs. Despite being hyper-focused on getting the right shot, I will never forget the furious sound of those many hooves and the way the ground trembled as they thundered from one end of the field to the other.

It was in Nevada that I got my first glimpse of truly wild horses. The Virginia Range outside Carson City is home to an estimated nine hundred horses, relatives of those that first inspired Wild Horse Annie's crusade. They were the first wild horses to be protected, when (thanks to Annie's campaigning) the 1952 Storey County law was passed prohibiting the poisoning of water holes and the use of aircraft to capture wild horses. Ironically, however, when the 1971 Wild Free-Roaming Horse and Burro Act was passed, these horses were not protected because they were not on federal land. Given that much of the Virginia Range is privately owned, the BLM determined that the area was not suitable for the long-term management of feral horses and instigated a capture program. Horses that remained in or entered the Virginia Range after this fell under state legislation pertaining to "estray" livestock, which is by law deemed the property of the Nevada Department of Agriculture until such time as the legal owner is identified or the animal is otherwise placed. Captured horses from the Virginia Range are taken to the Nevada Department of Agriculture's holding facility in Carson City, located at the Northern Nevada Correctional Facility. The horses are kept there for up to sixty days to allow sufficient opportunity for adoption and placement. Estray horses that have not been adopted by the end of the sixty-day period are offered for public sale at the holding facility; remaining horses are transported and sold to the highest bidder at a livestock auction.

Horses are usually captured or rounded up when they begin to encroach on a congested residential or commercial area or when the reduction of herd numbers is considered essential to maintaining a healthy and sustainable horse population in the range. Yet in one neighborhood, Virginia City Highlands, many Nevada mustangs are left to roam free. Perched at an elevation of 6200 feet (1890 meters) at the base of the Sierra Nevada Mountains, this community has become famous for the horses that meander around the yards, hills, and twisting roads of the semi-rural neighborhood. Driving down the main street, I encountered a stallion and two of his mares crossing from a semi-forested area to a resident's yard, where the family's domestic horse was housed in a street-facing corral. The mustangs showed a lot of interest in the domestic and walked right up to the fencing, which made the owned horse become very agitated and begin to buck and sprint around the pen. The stallion, unsure whether I posed a threat or not, hung back, keeping a constant eye on my car. Finally he consented to let me pass.

In the Highlands, residents have wild horse license plates and mailboxes and novelty signs bearing such phrases as "Caution! Wild Horse Crossing." They are clearly proud to share their neighborhood with these historic creatures, but problems may arise when wild animals become too familiar. It is easy to begin to think of these inquisitive, majestic creatures as domestic pets. I was told that many well-intentioned people put food and water out for them or try to lure them closer and closer to their homes; children try to befriend them, touch them, or even tame them. Harmless as it sounds, it is potentially dangerous for people who are inexperienced with wild horses, and ultimately very bad for the horses, whose survival depends on the strength of their wild instincts.

Mike Holmes is the Virginia estray manager for the state of Nevada and is in charge of the Virginia Range mustangs. Mike is a soft-spoken Nevada native who grew up in Carson City during a time when kids often tried to rope mustangs, hoping to "break" them and keep them as domestics. He wears a cowboy hat and looks the part as, eyes peeled for horses, he drives his mobile office—a truck—around the rugged western Nevada landscape. The Virginia Range encompasses more than 283,000 acres (114,500 hectares), and in the winter, if you don't know where to look for horses, you're not likely to find them. As we were driving, Mike would spot tiny specks in the distant landscape, point, and say "Horse."

Fortunately, the bands we encountered stayed more or less in the same grazing areas for the next few days, allowing me to find them again and spend some time photographing them. As would be expected, these horses were much more skittish and fearful of humans than those in sanctuaries. None allowed me to get closer than a few hundred feet, and the stallions kept a very alert eye on me the whole time. One horse we spotted in a small band of about five head was wearing a bridle. Apparently, he was a domestic horse that had been purchased by a local man several years back, but after spotting the mustangs had escaped and joined them. Several attempts had been made at capturing him—all unsuccessful.

I also visited the holding pens at the Correctional Facility, where recently culled mustangs are held until they can be adopted out. Despite himself, Mike seems to have become very fond of the horses. He is very protective of them and even adopted a foal to which he became attached after administering medicine for months. During his tenure, not one captured wild horse has ever been sent to a livestock auction. This is an enormous accomplishment. Such nonprofit rescues as Lifesavers and Return to Freedom have taken many of Mike's horses, but as rescue groups run out of room and more and more horses need relocating, the future may not be so bright for Nevada estrays.

Some 3000 miles (4800 kilometers) away, around Corolla, North Carolina, one of the last remaining herds of Spanish mustangs lives among tourists and beach houses on the Outer Banks—land that has been the horses' home for five hundred years. The Outer Banks (the string of islands off the North Carolina coast) are a popular vacation destination, and, as the Currituck area became more developed in the 1980s and a paved highway was put in, horses began getting hit by cars. Several decades ago, the Corolla Wild Horse Fund was formed in order to protect the herd, working with several North Carolina state organizations to have 12,000 acres (4860 hectares) of the northernmost beaches, abutting the Virginia border, defined as a horse sanctuary. Today, the horses live in an area accessible only by driving along the beach in a 4x4 vehicle. Despite the remote location, or perhaps because of it, many people do in fact live in the horse territory, in rudimentary neighborhoods surrounding the nature preserve.

In the summer, owing to the heat and the need to escape insects, bands of mustangs run on the beach, wade in the sea, and frolic in the sand. In the winter, however, they are more concerned with grazing, and they do that quite often in people's yards. Some residents have put up fences in an attempt to save their grass or gardens from peril, but often the horses find a way in regardless. Again, most residents adore the horses, and many live in the area because of them, but there are some locals and officials who view them as pests and as an impediment to development.

In Corolla, there is a $500 fine for coming within 50 feet (15 meters) of a wild horse. This law was enacted after tourists were found braiding the horses' manes, feeding them sandwiches, and trying to lure them toward their cabins for photos. There is also a $500 penalty for killing a wild horse. When I was there, the Corolla Wild Horse Fund had recently found a dead stallion that had been shot. Ironically, though, hunting is allowed in both the NC Estuarine Research Reserve and the federal Currituck Wildlife Refuge. I saw several orange-clad hunters prowling the dunes, presumably in search of feral boar, in the early mornings while I was looking for horses. Although it is illegal to shoot a horse, it is almost inevitable that accidents will happen when hunting is mixed with conservation.

The preservation of the Corolla wild horses continues to be a battle, but the horses also draw big tourism dollars as families come from all over to get a glimpse of the famed mustangs. In the summer months, the tiny town welcomes up to 60,000 tourists a week. The Corolla Wild Horse Fund operates a small gift store and educational center in historic Corolla and works with several local companies to facilitate tours. You cannot hope even to catch sight of these animals without a 4x4 vehicle, as there are very few proper roads and access to the neighborhoods is gained only by driving over huge, loose sand dunes.

It's an adventure being jostled around in a Jeep, careening over dunes and tracking fresh horse poop in an effort to locate the wandering bands. I definitely felt we had earned it when we finally came upon our first group. The horses, although not used to being touched by people, are supremely accustomed to being gawked at and photographed. Some will amble slowly away, but most barely even stop chewing when they look up, acknowledge you, and then return to grazing.

Another ancient coastal herd inhabits the tiny island of Vieques, Puerto Rico. Vieques lies 8 miles (13 kilometers) east of the Puerto Rican mainland and is only 21 miles (34 kilometers) long by 4 miles (6.5 kilometers) wide; it was once used by the US Navy as a bombing range and weapons-testing ground. The island retains a strong Spanish feel resulting from Puerto Rico's four hundred years as a Spanish settlement. The large numbers of wild horses that inhabit Vieques are Paso Finos, descendants of the horses that invading conquistadores brought there in the first decades of the sixteenth century. Because of their geographical isolation, the bloodlines have remained relatively pure and have resulted in some of the most uniquely beautiful horses in the world.

Opposite: An adolescent boy rides a native Paso Fino bareback down the beach, using a switch as a whip. "Breaking" and then claiming one of the wild horses on the island of Vieques, Puerto Rico, is a common pastime for young men. The horses are given amateur brands to make it clear that they are "taken," but are still left to roam the island.

Any Viequen will tell you that these horses are all "owned"—that they are not wild. In fact, many horses do exhibit amateur brands that imply they have been "claimed" by a local for riding or breeding stock. "Claiming" a good horse carries with it a certain social status, and you will often see male islanders attempting to ride these animals through the narrow streets, grooming them at public stalls, or even bathing them in the ocean. However, owing to the lack of private grazing land and because of cultural norms, the majority of Viequen horses are more or less wild. They find their own food and water, breed at will, and roam the island completely unregulated. Many older horses have faded brands and marled manes, showing no recent sign of human intervention. Such animals were most likely claimed when they were young but left alone after their usefulness declined. Whether or not these horses have been "broken" at one time or another, they retain the demeanor of wild animals. Most allow people near enough to photograph them, but very few will approach or allow you to touch them.

Since none of the herds around the island seemed to have a distinct name, I decided to name them after where they hung out, since most stayed in or returned to the same spots day after day. You can't drive more than a mile without encountering horses. The largest herd we visited daily, which I dubbed the "Chapel herd," hung out in a field across from a strip of coast known as "gringo beach"; a small chapel near the water was (to non-natives) the only discernible landmark. After several days of observing the Viequen horses, we figured out that, although most herds ventured out to fields and grassy areas during the day to graze, at night they retreated to the labyrinths of intricate, narrow paths overgrown by vines, flowers, and vegetation winding through the many tropical forests on Vieques.

Every morning, we saw horses foraging through the garbage dumpsters at an apartment complex. This was a strange sight. On a central road that leads through town, we continually spotted them trotting across the parking lot of a cluster of brightly painted stucco apartment buildings. Then, on closer inspection, we noticed large horse behinds sticking out from the small shelters where residents dumped their garbage. One day, a mother and foal were munching from the bin. One had a discarded tub of guacamole, the other a used diaper. Suddenly, one morning when I approached them, the horses all took off running and we decided to follow them. Down the road a few blocks and behind the main building of what looked like a small factory or government office, they ran through a small gap in a fence and into a fantastic tropical forest. As we snuck slowly in after them, we saw that they were all grazing on vegetation and native fruit, which was abundant in the jungle. They did not forage in the dumpster out of necessity but rather through choice. It seemed to us that they had developed a taste for garbage as a change from fruit and leaves.

Food is plentiful on the island, the climate is warm all year, and Viequen horses largely have free run of the place. However, some of the "claiming" practices seem inhumane. I saw a man riding a clearly agitated mare down the paved center of town with her young foal clinging to her tail, desperately trying to keep up so that they would not get separated. It was very sad to witness and must have been enormously stressful to both mother and baby. Several very young foals, not even yearlings, had already been given brands. There is also very little money or initiative for medical care. Sick foals, often riddled with worms, are frequently left to starve. The Vieques Humane Society does everything it can to help these horses, as well as the many stray dogs and cats that populate the island, but funds are extremely limited. Many lame or injured horses, such as the mare on the cover of this book, who was suffering from an old leg injury, do not receive proper care. In one sense, this is the natural peril that wild animals face. Without humans to treat their illnesses or mend their wounds, animals heal themselves, perish naturally, or become prey. There are few natural predators of horses, and none other than humans (and their cars) exists in Vieques, so most horses live out their lives in relative safety. Personally, though, I feel that if humans have decided to use these animals, even briefly, for pleasure or status, then they have an obligation to treat any injuries or illnesses during that period as well as to cultivate a lasting concern for the general health and well-being of the stock as a whole.

The legendary horses of Chincoteague, so romantically immortalized in the *Misty* books, still exist. The celebrity herd is still managed by the Chincoteague Volunteer Fire Company, and every year, the famed Pony Swim, which began in 1925, draws more than 40,000 spectators, who throng to the shore to watch between 150 and 175 wild horses swim the Assateague Channel. The three-minute event is followed by a carnival and auction where young ponies born the previous year are auctioned to raise funds for the fire department and the management of the herd. The remaining ponies swim back to Assateague Island a few days later.

Assateague Island, on the border of Maryland and Virginia, is a National Park managed by three park agencies and home to two distinct herds of wild horses. A simple fence on the beach marks the border, and two separate entrances—one in Maryland, to Assateague Island National Seashore, and one in Virginia, to Chincoteague National Wildlife Refuge— grant visitors access to the unspoiled island. The Maryland side is home to about 130 wild ponies, who roam completely free in the National Seashore. Some small bands spend most of their time foraging for treats in the busier campgrounds. Usually, several horses can be spotted grazing on the main road along with deer, rabbits, and other wildlife, but most roam the remote dunes, beaches, swamps, and maritime forests of the park's 48,000 acres (19,425 hectares), most of which are reachable only by off-road vehicles.

I was fortunate to be given a personal tour by park staff Allison Turner, who spent the day driving me along the many miles of beach in search of the horses. The bands often stay in the same area for days or weeks at a time, which is very helpful, as horses generally blend well into the surrounding landscape and can be remarkably difficult to find. Generally, if you follow the poop and the hoofprints, you will eventually find them.

They were some of the most beautiful horses I have seen anywhere, and I was lucky to visit during a time of stallion unrest, when several stallions were being challenged for their mares and several others had just lost their bands. It is fascinating to watch these challenges, and even more amazing to photograph them. In reality, wild horses spend about 90 percent of their day grazing, barely even lifting their heads. They generally go on to the beach only to escape bugs; they gallop down the beach only in order to get from one place to another, or, often, to run from photographers; and except for young stallions, who tend to be very playful, there isn't much bucking and rearing unless there is some unrest. That particular week in Assateague, however, I saw at least three challenges.

Generally, a bachelor stallion would approach a band of mares. The stallion whose band it was would immediately run toward the intruder; the mares would huddle together, watching the action. The two stallions would gallop at each other and then stop. One would poop. The other would smell the poop. Then they usually

A mother and foal forage in a garbage bin at an apartment complex on Vieques, Puerto Rico.

19

began bucking and charging until one gave up (usually the challenger). The triumphant stallion would then run back to his mares and continue grazing, while keeping an eye out for another challenge. The bachelor would return to his territory and continue to roam and graze, either alone or with a small band of other bachelors.

Many smaller wild horse rescues and sanctuaries can be found all over the country. The chances are that if you want to see some of these creatures close up, you may not have to travel very far. I was excited to find that at least one such rescue existed near my home in New England: Ever After Mustang Rescue, one of coastal Maine's best-kept secrets. Driving by the small farm in Biddeford, you would never guess that most of the horses serenely grazing on the property were once galloping freely across the plains of the western United States. Founder Mona Jerome is extremely dedicated to taking in and rehabilitating mustangs that have come from neglectful and abusive homes, as well as some that she has directly saved from being sent to livestock auctions. It is all too common for wild horses to be bought at BLM auctions by well-intentioned people who end up not having the money, time, or patience to care for a mustang. In many cases, these horses are neglected if they are not re-homed. Although Mona encourages adoption at her farm, many of the mustangs she cares for are too old to be of interest to most adopters, and will spend the rest of their days at the rescue. Funds are always tight, and Mona spends every day from dawn until dusk caring for the animals. She also runs a program where local "at risk" youth come to the farm as volunteers. The kids help out with chores and work directly with gentled mustangs. Those with whom I spoke seemed to have acquired a real reverence for the horses, and I had to wonder if maybe they felt a kinship with them, because horses and humans shared the experience of a tumultuous or even abusive past.

Mona Jerome, founder of Ever After Mustang Rescue, Maine, with one of the many rescued mustangs she trains and cares for.

Wild horses still exist in America, but in varying states of freedom. There are many corners of horse country that I was unable to visit, but my aim was to create a cohesive picture representing the current different conditions of mustangs around the country. Many herds, such as the Assateague Island and

Puerto Rican horses, are constrained only by the geographical barriers of the islands on which they live, while others, such as the Corolla horses, live in government-sanctioned preserve lands with fenced-in boundaries. Tens of thousands of others from Nevada and nine other western states are in federal holding pens or privately owned sanctuaries; and then there exists a minority that is still actually free. Every day these horses face the possibility of capture and removal. As rescues run out of room, and development continues to encroach on the remaining lands and threaten the environments where these animals thrive, we as Americans will have to find new ways of preserving and protecting the unique heritage embodied in these beautiful animals. Solutions must be found through legislation, increased awareness and education, and the financial support of rescue groups. These horses, just like our national parks and our oceans, belong to us all—and so it falls to every concerned citizen to protect them and ensure that they are here for another five hundred years.

A wild horse naps at the entrance to Assateague Island National Seashore, Maryland, a park that receives millions of visitors every year. Several bands of horses live and graze year round in the public campgrounds and more developed areas of the park.

"They are worth keeping alive not just because they exist,
but also because they are extraordinary."

Steve Edwards, Corolla Wild Horse Fund board member, natural horse trainer,
and owner of seven formerly wild Corolla Mustangs

WILD Horses

The first is Freddy, on the hill with the burros. Freddy arrived in 1999
with the Hart Mountain horses—the first band to arrive at the Return to
Freedom American Wild Horse Sanctuary in Lompoc, California. They
were gathered in what was a "total removal" of 279 horses from the U.S.
Fish & Wildlife Service Hart Mountain Refuge in Oregon. The burros came
from the Fish & Wildlife Service Sheldon Refuge in Nevada.

Brave Heart, a handsome, bold eleven-year-old from
Ever After Mustang Rescue in Maine.

A mare, part of the Corolla herd in the Outer Banks region of
North Carolina, looks up suspiciously while grazing.

Diamond, a beautiful three-year-old filly from
Oregon's Hart Mountain herd.

Chief Iktinike, a pure Choctaw stallion (a strain of the Spanish Colonial Mission horses),
and his main mare, Nightcamp, at the Return to Freedom Sanctuary. These horses are from
Blackjack Mountain, Oklahoma; horses there are currently being rounded up and removed.

A stallion in the "Chapel herd" is alerted to my presence
while grazing in a field next to a main road on the island
of Vieques, Puerto Rico.

A mare from the "Chapel herd" on Vieques grazes in the early-morning
sun. Many of the horses here are amateurly branded by islanders who
have claimed them as their own either for recreation or for breeding
stock. Despite this loose "ownership," the horses are generally left to
roam, graze, and breed freely on the island.

Isis is one of the 150 pregnant or newly foaled mares rescued from the Fish Creek Ranch in Nevada (see also page 100). The herd was purchased from two Shoshone women, who had captured them from the wild. Most were moved to a California ranch, but the heavy mares and young foals were left in a small corral to be moved at a later date. However, the new owner never retrieved them and they were found starving to death. Forty-seven lives were lost before the survivors were rescued. Isis now lives at the Lifesavers Born to Be Wild sanctuary in California.

"They have roamed the marshes, maritime forests,
and beaches of the Outer Banks for 500 years.
My goal is to ensure their health and safety for
500 more. It is a lofty goal."

Karen McCalpin, Director, Corolla Wild Horse Fund, North Carolina

Laredo is a nine-year-old gelding who was captured
by the Bureau of Land Management and now lives at
the Lifesavers ranch in Lancaster, California.

A small band of Virginia Range mustangs in Nevada.

This mare was part of a group that we dubbed the "Garbage herd" because they would emerge every morning from their lush jungle home to forage in the overflowing garbage dumps at a nearby apartment community on Vieques, Puerto Rico.

A young bay, part of the last remaining herd of Spanish mustangs
on the northern Outer Banks, grazes in Corolla, North Carolina.

Sage, now living at the Lifesavers Born to Be Wild sanctuary near Caliente, California, came from the Virginia Range near Reno, Nevada, and is one of the horses that Wild Horse Annie (real name Velma Johnston) fought so hard to protect. It was Wild Horse Annie's campaign that finally led to the Wild Free-Roaming Horse and Burro Act of 1971.

"I think the only hope we have to preserve
natural herds, or even individual born-wild horses,
is to relocate them to private lands where
they can live without government interference."

Jill Starr, Founder, Lifesavers Wild Horse Rescue, California

This very underweight colt from the "Chapel herd" on Vieques,
Puerto Rico, probably suffers from worms, which are a
common threat to young wild mustangs.

Mirage (left), Elvis (second from right), and Tyler (right; also pictured on page 68) munch on fresh hay at the Lifesavers Lancaster ranch.

Jasmine (left) and Sage at the Lifesavers Born to Be Wild sanctuary near Caliente,
California. Both are from Nevada: Jasmine from the Fish Creek rescue operation
(see pages 35 and 100) and Sage from the Virginia Range near Reno. Virginia
Range horses are captured by the state when they become nuisances and endanger
themselves or others by crossing or standing in the roads.

"The plight of the wild horse, climate change, and the rapid depletion of our natural resources are all indicators that our world is out of balance. We desperately need a shift in conscious awareness, to reconnect to our community and our planet and trust in our better selves."

Jill Anderson, Director of Development and Communications,
Return to Freedom American Wild Horse Sanctuary, California

Mirage and Elvis. Mirage (the buckskin, foreground) is from the Fish Creek herd in Nevada (see pages 35 and 100). Elvis is a Bureau of Land Management mustang whose history is something of a mystery: someone bought him at auction, and after several people tried unsuccessfully to ride him, he was passed around to a few homes. His last owners surrendered him to Lifesavers, since they have more experience with mustangs.

A stallion and one of his mares, part of the Virginia Range estray herd in Nevada, are startled by me in a Carson City field.

Antonia Cruce (see also page 73), a Spanish Colonial Mission mare from the Wilbur-Cruce herd, now lives at the Return to Freedom Sanctuary. For more information on this herd, see page 121.

A blue-eyed mustang on Vieques, Puerto Rico.

A chestnut mare and her foal relax in the tall grass near a housing development outside Carson City, Nevada.

An older Viequen mare in Puerto Rico.

Affectionately referred to as the "three amigos," these are three of fifteen burros that arrived at Return to Freedom, California, from the U.S. Fish & Wildlife Service Sheldon Refuge in Nevada. Return to Freedom currently cares for a total of twenty-eight burros.

"Clearly the American mustang is the underdog
of the horse world. Widely misunderstood, and
almost always mishandled in captivity, it has an
undeserved reputation for being difficult
and unmanageable."

Jill Starr, Founder, Lifesavers Wild Horse Rescue, California

A small band of mustangs runs through the arid brush in the Virginia Range area of Nevada. Horses that live there are considered "estray" livestock and are deemed the property of the Nevada Department of Agriculture until their owners are found, or until they are adopted or sold.

Hart Mountain and Sheldon horses wait for the feed truck on a stormy morning at the Return to Freedom Sanctuary, California.

Sabre, a five-year-old mare, tells the others to get behind her as she waits for feed on this rainy morning at Return to Freedom, California. These mustangs came from the Hart Mountain Refuge in Oregon.

Crimson, one of the rescued Fish Creek mares (see pages 35 and 100), yawns in the early morning at the Lifesavers Born to Be Wild sanctuary near Caliente, California.

A lovely older mare on Vieques, Puerto Rico—one of what we called the "Chapel herd" because their grazing site was near a seaside chapel. Her left front leg is lame, probably because of an untreated injury.

Thoroughbred Naveau (opposite) was an old grand prix jumper. When her owner died, the family surrendered her to Lifesavers in Lancaster, California. Most wild horse rescue centers also periodically take in horses that are not mustangs as an alternative to slaughter.

A blue-eyed Spanish Barb mustang on Vieques, Puerto Rico.

Two stallions charge into another stallion's territory on Assateague Island, Maryland.

Competing stallions begin a confrontation on the beach on Assateague Island, Maryland.

A buckskin mustang rests during the heat of the day in the Vieques beachside public campground Sun Bay, which is home to a large herd of between fifteen and thirty mustangs.

Tyler is a Bureau of Land Management mustang about twelve years old, and had a significant amount of training before ending up at the Lifesavers Lancaster ranch. His previous owners invested a lot of time and money in him; however, he likes to buck. His bucking certainly seems to be fear-based, and when in an uncomfortable or frightening situation, he reverts to the prey animal way of thinking that is at the core of his being. For now, he is just being allowed to clear his mind and be a horse, and soon his potential for continued training or release will be evaluated.

Patience is a six-year-old mare from Virginia City, Nevada. Lifesavers received her in 2007 along with her foal, Honesty. Patience and eight other pairs of mothers and foals were part of a contraception study carried out by one of the universities. As the mares had their foals, they were booted out of the program; many were allowed back into the wild. But when this group's time came to be released, there was a mountain lion in the area and the wranglers at the Virginia City facility were worried about the foals, so the horses were brought to the Lifesavers Lancaster ranch instead. Patience is the most gentle and docile of the group.

"There are already twenty vacation homes for every horse. I fear that we will soon develop them out of existence."

Karen McCalpin, Director, Corolla Wild Horse Fund, North Carolina

A foal and his mother at the Carson City holding center at the Northern Nevada Correctional Facility. Mustangs that have been rounded up from surrounding land are kept here for sixty days, after which time they are released, adopted, or put up for public sale or auction. Though the state has the authority to sell these horses to the kill auctions, so far not a single one has been sold, because rescue groups have managed to find homes for them. However, the state is removing them in larger numbers now, and the rescue groups are running out of room.

Antonia Cruce, one of the original mares from the Wilbur–Cruce Spanish Colonial Mission herd, now at the Return to Freedom Sanctuary in California (see also page 50).

Portrait of a bold stallion who chased me away from his mares several times. Like many other horses on the island of Vieques, Puerto Rico, he has many burrs in his mane from grazing in the mangroves. (See also page 93.)

A stallion crosses a dirt road in the isolated coastal community of Corolla, North Carolina. With few remaining, the Colonial Spanish Mustang is listed as a critically threatened breed.

A young bay mustang at Return to Freedom, California.

Paloma is a beautiful palomino mare, who arrived at Return to Freedom pregnant, very underweight, and malnourished, after being held in the Bureau of Land Management pens. She gave birth to Franchesca Rose (pictured on page 82) at the sanctuary, where the two now spend their days together.

Part of a large herd that lives on 20 acres (8 hectares)

at the Lifesavers ranch in Lancaster, California.

A horse grazes in the marshland at the Assateague

Island National Seashore in Maryland.

"The American wild horse is rapidly disappearing. The Colonial Spanish Mustang carries a wealth of ancient genetic history, and we must do everything possible to conserve the breed, as its ancestors from Spain are now extinct."

Karen McCalpin, Director, Corolla Wild Horse Fund, North Carolina

Three mustangs follow a path to water in Corolla, North Carolina, where they roam 12,000 protected acres (4855 hectares) of coastal land.

Franchesca Rose was born at Return to Freedom from Paloma (pictured on page 77), who was rounded up late in her pregnancy and was not doing well. Mother and daughter are inseparable.

*Two young mustangs from the "Chapel herd" play on the beach
on Vieques, Puerto Rico.*

A herd at the Lifesavers Born to Be Wild sanctuary near Caliente, California, awaits its early-morning feeding.

A mare pauses in her grazing in the shade of thick jungle at the side

of a steep, winding mountain road on Vieques, Puerto Rico.

Mustangs run together in their large corral at the Carson City,
Nevada, holding facility. Horses are captured when they stray
into residential or commercial areas or on to roadways, where
they pose a hazard.

Red, a handsome, stocky stallion from Hart Mountain, Oregon.
He was one of the first stallions to arrive at Return to Freedom,
California, when the U.S. Fish & Wildlife Service removed all
the wild horses from the Hart Mountain Refuge in 1998.

Two mares are hurried away by a stallion on
Assateague Island, Maryland.

A young, blue-eyed chestnut stallion on
Assateague Island, Maryland.

Franco (right) and one of the three amigos (see page 54) at Return to Freedom, California. The three amigos are so named because they are often found together and, with the humor and intelligence that characterize burros, frequently strike wonderful poses.

A stallion from the "Chapel herd" on Vieques, Puerto Rico.

(See also page 74.)

These are just a few of the mares rescued from such situations as the Bureau of Land Management sale authority and the Nevada estray program, or from starvation, abuse, neglect, or surrender. These horses are not suitable for adoption because they are too old, unsound, or mentally unstable; or in some cases they have been abused and simply deserve peace and quiet at the Lifesavers Born to Be Wild sanctuary near Caliente, California.

This young mare was part of the "Garbage herd" (see page 39) on Vieques, Puerto Rico, and is shown here back in the safety of the intricate maze of lush jungle trails.

A chestnut bachelor stallion on the beach on Assateague

Island, Maryland.

Another chestnut bachelor stallion stretches following an afternoon rest on Assateague Island, Maryland.

A skittish young mare from the "Chapel herd" runs

from me on Vieques, Puerto Rico.

Another mustang from the "Chapel herd" on Vieques, Puerto Rico.

The wild horses of Vieques are descendants of the horses that the Spanish

conquistadores brought to the island in the early sixteenth century.

Venice was saved from the Fish Creek Ranch in Nevada (see also page 35). A pregnant mare, she miscarried her foal because of the terrible stress and starvation she had to endure prior to being rescued by Lifesavers.

The Shoshone-owned herd was rounded up by helicopter by the Bureau of Land Management in February 2003 after a thirty-year dispute over grazing rights finally came to an end. Yet the month of February is the beginning of foaling season, and foaling season is the worst time to gather horses, especially by helicopter, as it is so frightening and physically demanding. The heavy mares have to run for miles before getting to rest in the trap. Those with newborns are in such a panic that many babies are left behind, unable to keep up with the stampeding herd, or trampled in the confusion.

On this occasion, the 150 horses were then left to starve in an overcrowded stock corral, so it was no wonder that a great many of these pregnant mares miscarried.

Part of a herd at the Lifesavers Born to Be Wild ranch near Caliente, California, sprints in anticipation of a morning feed.

Members of the "Chapel herd" run along the coast of Vieques,
Puerto Rico, as a beach-goer cools off in the background.

Two horses share a close moment at Return to Freedom
in California.

A band of mustangs takes time out to roll in the

warm sand on Assateague Island, Maryland.

Christobol, a mature Curly stallion (a breed of mustang with very soft, curly hair similar to mohair), was captured in Wyoming and now lives at Return to Freedom, California.

An older mare at Return to Freedom, California.

A mustang at the Lifesavers Lancaster ranch enjoys a mid-afternoon

roll in the dirt.

A Virginia Range estray pinto stands guard in a field in Nevada.

Two young bachelors play at Return to Freedom, California.

A young pinto colt on Vieques, Puerto Rico, soothes an itch.

Chief Iktinike (left) and Red Creek of a Choctaw band at Return to Freedom, California. Chief is the stallion. (See also pages 30 and 31.)

Three members of a beautiful herd we found grazing in an

abandoned beachfront lot near our house on Vieques, Puerto Rico.

BJ (left) and Cabo. BJ is not a mustang: he is a registered Paint, surrendered to the Lifesavers Lancaster ranch because of family hardship. Although not a wild horse, he is a very challenging one.

"Wild free-roaming horses belong to no
one individual. They belong to all the American
people.... The spirit which has kept them alive and
free against almost insurmountable odds typifies
the national spirit which led to the growth of our Nation.
They are living symbols of the rugged independence
and tireless energy of our pioneer heritage."

U.S. Senate Report No. 242, 92nd Congress, 1971

On Vieques, Puerto Rico, a watchful mother eyes me

as her newborn filly moves closer to her side.

A muscular chestnut stallion pauses in front of palm trees lining a beach on Vieques, Puerto Rico.

Diamonte Cruce, a stunning Spanish Barb stallion from the Wilbur–Cruce Spanish Colonial Mission

herd, now at the Return to Freedom Sanctuary, California. These classic Spanish Barb horses are

descendants of the original horses brought to the Americas in the late seventeenth century by Padre

Kino, who brought the best ranch horses from Spain to his headquarters, the famed Mission Delores

in Sonora, Mexico. In the nineteenth century, Dr. Reuben Wilbur purchased a herd of these horses,

which roamed his ranch in southern Arizona for a hundred years, until the land's sale in 1990 by

Wilbur's granddaughter Eva Cruce. Diamonte's parents both came from the Wilbur–Cruce ranch.

A Kiger mustang colt at Return to Freedom, California. The Kiger breed,
which is usually dun with dark points and markings, was discovered during
a Bureau of Land Management round-up in Oregon in the 1970s.

A mare pauses for me on Vieques, Puerto Rico, as the sun is setting.

Blondie (running in front) was rescued from a feed lot in Washington. She is about thirteen years old, rideable, and an absolute sweetheart. Blondie came with a note attached, claiming that she was a nice horse but had sudden and inexplicable bouts of violence. Staff at the Lifesavers Lancaster ranch have never witnessed any such behavior and say that she is a joy to work with.

Tatonka, a handsome Spanish mustang with unusual markings, was born at Return to Freedom, California, after his parents were captured on Navajo lands in New Mexico and sold at auction for 10 cents a pound.

A band of wild horses on Assateague Island,

Maryland, turns to watch me.

Horses scatter as a new stallion challenges for dominance

of this band of mares on Assateague Island, Maryland.

Hopi and his son Maka Maza Zi are Spanish mustangs from Navajo lands. Hopi and Maka Maza Zi's mother, Shoshona, were rounded up and sold at auction for 10 cents a pound. The three now live peacefully at Return to Freedom, California.

129

Hopi and Maka Maza Zi at Return to Freedom, California

(see previous page).

A black stallion gallops down the beach on Assateague Island, Maryland.

Four stallions challenge one another on Assateague Island, Maryland.

On Vieques, Puerto Rico, one of the "Sun Bay herd," a striking young
mustang with very light-brown eyes, pauses briefly from grazing.

A young mustang at Ever After Mustang Rescue in Maine. Ever After offers rescue, rehabilitation, and adoption, primarily for previously adopted mustangs. It also works with "at risk" young people, providing hands-on opportunities to work with the horses.

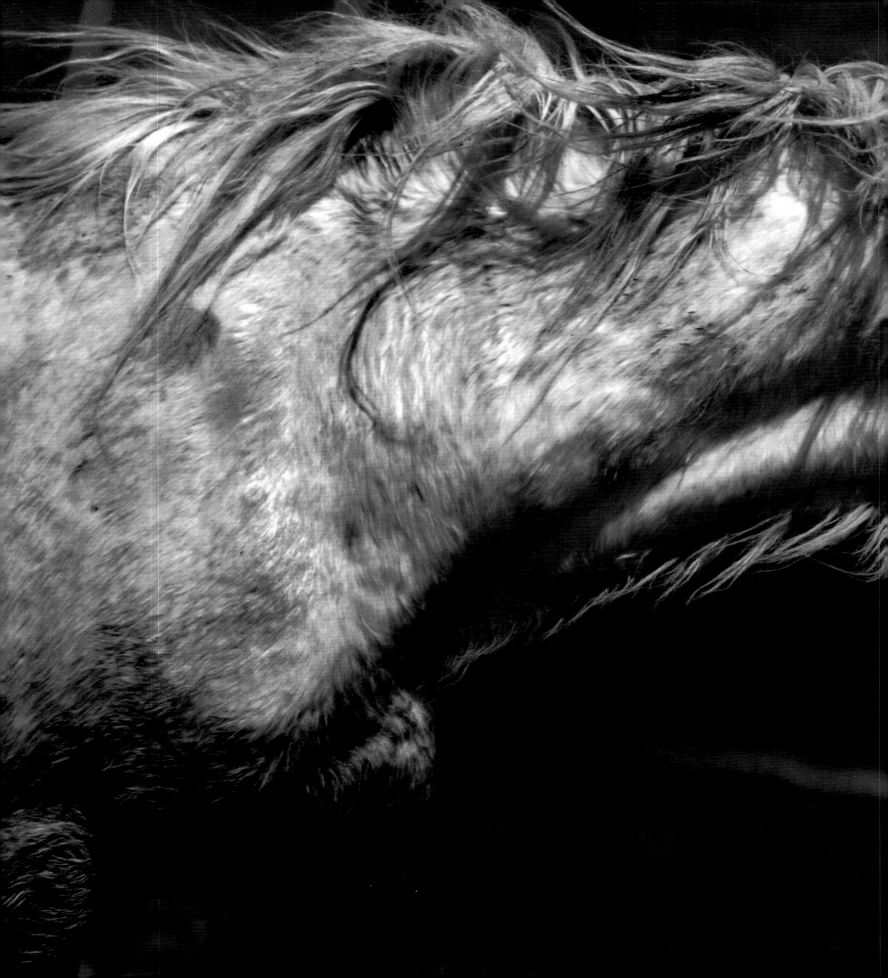

Foxfire is twenty-two years old and was surrendered to Ever After Mustang Rescue, Maine, when her young owner left for college.

Skittish, small Half Pint was purchased at an auction in
Skowhegan, Maine, in 2003, to save him from being sent to
slaughter in Canada. He is now eleven years old and up for
adoption at Ever After Mustang Rescue, Maine.

A couple of two-year-olds from the Hart Mountain herd, now at Return to Freedom, California. In 1998, all wild horses were removed from Hart Mountain, Oregon, a wildlife refuge managed by the U.S. Fish & Wildlife Service.

Two stallions battle over a band of mares on Assateague Island, Maryland.

"America's wild horses represent the rugged and independent spirit of this nation. Tragically, they are disappearing from our Western landscape. Because of an ongoing and aggressive wild horse removal policy, there are now more wild horses living in captivity than remain in the wild."

Jill Anderson, Director of Development and Communications,
Return to Freedom American Wild Horse Sanctuary, California

RESCUE AND CONSERVATION GROUPS

AMERICAN WILD HORSE PRESERVATION CAMPAIGN

The American Wild Horse Preservation Campaign is supported by a broad-based coalition of public-interest groups, environmentalists, humane organizations, and historical societies, representing more than 10 million supporters.

wildhorsepreservation.org

P.O. Box 926, Lompoc, CA 93438

877-853-4696

ASSATEAGUE ISLAND NATIONAL SEASHORE FOSTER HORSE PROGRAM

The Assateague Island National Seashore Foster Horse Program offers horse lovers and beach lovers a meaningful way to contribute to the Maryland herd's upkeep and to habitat projects that sustain the environment.

assateaguewildhorses.org

P.O. Box 731, Berlin, MD 21811

410-629-1538

BLACK HILLS WILD HORSE SANCTUARY

The Black Hills Wild Horse Sanctuary comprises 11,000 acres (4450 hectares) of land, which not only allows freedom for more than 500 horses but also incorporates a research area dedicated to solving wild horse herd management that will contribute to the well-being of all wild horses.

wildmustangs.com

P.O. Box 998, Hot Springs, SD 57747

800-252-6652 or 605-745-5955

COROLLA WILD HORSE FUND

The mission of the Corolla Wild Horse Fund is to protect, preserve, and manage responsibly the herd of wild Colonial Spanish mustangs roaming freely on the northernmost Currituck Outer Banks, and to promote the continued preservation of this land as a permanent sanctuary for horses defined as a cultural treasure by the state of North Carolina.

corollawildhorses.com

P.O. Box 361, 1126 Old Schoolhouse Lane, Corolla, NC 27927

252-453-8002

EVER AFTER MUSTANG RESCUE

Ever After rescues and rehabilitates previously adopted mustangs that have suffered from neglect or abuse and/or are facing slaughter, and helps to place them in loving homes. Visitors are welcome by appointment.

mustangrescue.org

463 West Street, Biddeford, ME 04005

207-284-7721

FOUNDATION FOR SHACKLEFORD HORSES

The foundation's mission is to protect and preserve the Shackleford Banks wild horses of North Carolina and ensure that their place in history is maintained in the future.

shacklefordhorses.org
306 Golden Farm Road, Beaufort, NC 28516
252-728-6308

LET 'EM RUN FOUNDATION

A nonprofit organization in partnership with government, business, and community for the protection and preservation of wild horses and the heritage of the American West.

letemrun.com
820 Cartwright Road, Virginia City Highlands, NV 89521
775-847-4777

LIFESAVERS WILD HORSE RESCUE

Lifesavers Wild Horse Rescue is dedicated to saving abandoned, abused, neglected, and slaughter-bound American mustangs through rescue, adoption, education, and sanctuary.

wildhorserescue.org
23809 East Avenue J, Lancaster, CA 93535
661-727-0049

RETURN TO FREEDOM
AMERICAN WILD HORSE SANCTUARY

Return to Freedom is dedicated to preserving the freedom, diversity, and habitat of America's wild horses through sanctuary, education, and conservation, while enriching the human spirit through direct experience with the natural world.

returntofreedom.org
P.O. Box 926, Lompoc, CA 93438
805-737-9246

VIEQUES HUMANE SOCIETY & ANIMAL RESCUE

The mission of the society is to relieve the suffering of the animals on the island of Vieques, Puerto Rico.

viequeshs.org
P.O. Box 1399, Vieques, PR 00765
787-741-0209

VIRGINIA RANGE WILDLIFE PROTECTION ASSOCIATION

The association works to preserve and protect all species of wildlife on the Virginia Range in Nevada.

vrwpa.org
P.O. Box 536, Virginia City, NV 89440
775-881-2288

Acknowledgments

I should like to give my sincerest thanks to everyone who helped in the making of this book. Through welcoming me into your homes, getting up at dawn to help me get that "one shot," helping with identification and captions, and sharing your expertise and dedication, you have truly made this possible: Jill Anderson, Matthew Bershadker, Neda DeMayo, Christine Driscoll, Mike Holmes, Karen McCalpin, Shannon Schureman, Jill Starr, Allison Turner, Chris and Martin Vilmer, and everyone at Lifesavers, Return to Freedom, Corolla Wild Horse Fund, and Amigos de los Animales P.R.

*A portion of the proceeds from sales of this book
will benefit the ASPCA* Equine Fund*
*The American Society for the Prevention of Cruelty to Animals®

First published 2008 by
Merrell Publishers Limited

81 Southwark Street
London SE1 0HX

merrellpublishers.com

Text and illustrations copyright © 2008 Traer Scott
Design and layout copyright © 2008 Merrell Publishers Limited

All rights reserved. No part of this publication may be reproduced, stored in a retrieval system, or transmitted, in any form or by any means, electronic, mechanical, photocopying, recording, or otherwise, without the prior permission in writing from the publisher.

British Library Cataloguing-in-Publication data:
Scott, Traer
Wild horses : endangered beauty
  1. Wild horses – North America
  I. Title
  599.6.655.097

ISBN-13: 978-1-8589-4463-0
ISBN-10: 1-8589-4463-5

For additional information on Traer Scott,
please visit traerscott.com

Produced by Merrell Publishers Limited
Designed by 3&Co.
Copy-edited by Kirsty Seymour-Ure
Proof-read by Kate Michell

Printed and bound in China

Jacket, front: An older mare on Vieques, Puerto Rico (see pages 62 and 63).
Jacket, back: Two young bachelors play at Return to Freedom, California (top left; see page 111); a young mare in Corolla, North Carolina (center); mustangs at the Carson City, Nevada, holding facility (top right; see page 88); two mustangs on the beach on Vieques, Puerto Rico (center right; see page 84); Foxfire, a mare at Ever After Mustang Rescue, Maine (bottom right; see also pages 136–37); BJ and Cabo, Lifesavers Lancaster ranch (bottom left; see page 116).
Frontispiece: A lone pinto stallion on Assateague Island, Maryland.
Page 4: A bay mare watches as the stallion of the herd defends the band against two challenging stallions on Assateague Island.
Pages 6–7: A newborn foal and her mother on Vieques, Puerto Rico.
Page 22: Two horses from the Hart Mountain herd; see page 139.
Page 24: A young mustang at Ever After Mustang Rescue, Maine; see page 135.